FROM MY HEART, TO HIS, TO PAPER

Maku Pamei

ISBN 978-93-5458-831-0
© Maku Pamei 2021
Published in India 2021 by Pencil

Contributors:
Editor: Merasen-na Jamir
Illustrator: Mannyei Phom

A brand of
One Point Six Technologies Pvt. Ltd.
123, Building J2, Shram Seva Premises,
Wadala Truck Terminal, Wadala (E)
Mumbai 400037, Maharashtra, INDIA
E connect@thepencilapp.com
W www.thepencilapp.com

All rights reserved worldwide

Author biography

Maku Pamei, is a twenty two year old from Dimapur, Nagaland. *From My Heart, To His, To Paper* is her first poetry book which she has been working and writing for the past one year.

It is a collection of poetry that talks about the process of finding someone to love, to loving, and finally to losing them in the end. She hopes to reach out to people through her work and wishes to write more in the future. She is currently pursuing her Masters in English from Assam Don Bosco University,Guwahati.

CONTENTS

Love is a Dagger

Love is a dagger,

but love is beautiful,

and if it ends,

It ends bitterly.

Glue me back together

Like broken glass on the sea shore, it looks pretty in it's own way.

Yet like broken promises,

None of it can be fixed again.

What it said

And the heart said,

It has to be forever

But it never was.

So

So maybe, she smells like emotions

Yet you say you can't smell feelings

So you don't really see her care,

And she lays soft as cotton,

Yet you say her edges are rough

so she doesn't deserve your happiness?

The Things You Said

Every tear that rolled down my cheek

Because of your name and all that you were,

Every single time you said goodbye,

Just for you to crash my peace again,

I hope it haunts you as much as it haunted me,

All the things you said before you half-left

As many times as you come back for me,

I hope karma repeats itself with her journey.

Until The End, You Lied

Your face sculptutred with such fine detail,

You looked like the finest piece of art

No one knew of the mud that laid inside

And while every visitor loved your grace,

My hands were shaking trying to fix you.

But who told me that I had to mend you?

Thought nobody would leave because I never told them,

I also never told you I could leave you alone forever.

Because until the very end, You lied to me, to them, and to Yourself.

To Forgive You

To forgive is virtue,

But to forgive you

I wonder how many times do I have to,

Until you realised what you did to us.

I Tried to find your Words

I have all the words to write for you,

But I could never figure out,

Despite all the tries I never found meaning,

In your *I Love Yous* and *I Will Never Let You go.*

Forever

Forever is a word you abused,

Like death, you came and took off

But death stays forever.

I had a Dream

In a place named after you,

Every scenery had your face painted,

The smell of diesel reminded me of my dream

Then it reminded me of you,

That sometimes dreams can end.

Colors

Each color symbolises something,

Yet if I had to define them

Would it be what sadness look like?

It was all Red

I asked you to show me the way to the stars,

But all you led me was to a staircase full of red.

Ctrl plus Delete

The story ends here,

Maybe it had to end somewhere.

Because I started writing and you kept pressing the backspace.

Waving

Someday you may need me,

You will need me, I am sure.

And I will be there despite it all,

But maybe you won't recognise me,

Maybe you will never see her again.

Now

Grieving for the past,

Longing for the future,

But I am still stuck in the middle

of what to do and where to go.

I Wonder What You Are

How do you ask yourself why?

When all you asked despite *hellos*

Was for him to act like he is human.

I Will Not

I cannot blame the world for what it is,

I cannot blame time for what it does,

And I will not blame myself for loving you.

Even though you turn out not to love me.

If Misery had a Name

What it meant losing you,

I don't know the loss,

But I know the package that came along.

How every night I could hear you,

Inside my mind and in my dreams,

How I would suddenly crumble down in tears.

It misery had a name, you would carry it well.

Lessons

I guess it's a thing with people

That they decide to choose

All the people that never cared,

Or walk anywhere but near the person,

Who taught them how to stand on their feet and walk.

Even the Wind Would Never do that

Like the wind, all of what you said flew away

Not softly, but in the harshest way possible.

You turned your promises into a sorry forever.

When You Left

Everything was empty. I felt nothing.

I gave you too much of me,

For a love so less which wasn't even true,

This is the part where I don't blame you.

This is a part I will take back no matter the cost,

For I know you can't even pay back.

You Left Since the Beginning

Ensuring all of the good things of the past now,

I realised none of it was ever to be with you.

I sigh in Dilemma

Isn't it ridiculous how we keep saying we are all okay even when we are anything but that?

To run away would be an act of cowardice, to face it would be too much.

If this is a part of life when will the next chapter unfold?

Wishes

Like a river that never runs dry and flows,

I wish my heart would feel the peace it once had.

Comfort

The Winter may have been harsh, but you know ever since your hand was on mine,

I have only known comfort.

So Far

You say you don't want to lose the bond,

But I have been trying so hard to understand

Why you keep going so far away from me?

After All That Is Said and Done

You kept talking of this hope to me,

Like that was all that you ever knew of,

Even when you left, could you have talked about the good things?

While you pretend to be strangers, there was nothing you knew of.

The Ghost of You

Each time I try to march on my parade,

The trumpets stop beacuse your siren blows.

Every time a new leaf grows, your dead leaves fall,

Almost as if you never want me to forget,

That you were once a part of me.

If I May

A new year will befall all of us,

But now all I will remember is,

How it was in the beginning we decided to end.

No each New Year is a reminder to me.

For a little while, for some years,

Let me think of you.

The Hurting

The difference is all bright and clear,

I hurt like I am lake trying to form into an ocean ,

 Each day like it is a thousand year,

While you sip in tea and play your court,

To you even a day is less.

From His Heart

I wonder if I could write what your heart feels,

But this is like I am Cheating,

Maybe to you I am a player of a hundred words,

Because your words are not mine to write,

And I could fantasize a lot but I could never be what you write,

To My Heart

My heart is like a little tape,

Every day it plays a little tune,

Some times it is off chorus

Somedays like a kind lovable chord

While there are moments of deepy agony and irritation

A series of what I could never describe.

To Paper

I am ink on different formats,

You will never know because I can never show.

The essence it carries is not mine but yours to keep.

The deeper you dig into my paper, you shall know.

That it is yours but also mine.

My paper is poetry, but It is also something I don't know.

Au Revoir

Everything I write, it's for you.

Every pain from the inch of my heart includes,

For I am tired of the things you do.

Read every single line of my poems,

You will know how much I have suffered.

Each day of my life without a single word

But a word of letters made me strong enough to say it out but for the whole world.

www.ingramcontent.com/pod-product-compliance
Lightning Source LLC
LaVergne TN
LVHW050427160726

843469LV00041B/1263